Joan von Ehren

Joan's Jungle

Memories of a Ms.-Manager

Mit einem Vorwort von
Dr. Jürgen Bruns

und 25 Vignetten von
Imke Kretzmann

ROSENFELD

Frankfurt am Main / München

"TRAINFO-JOAN" UNPLUGGED

Ein Germane sucht nach einer unkonventionellen Möglichkeit, sein kümmerliches Englisch auf „a higher level of excellence" (was ist das bloß?!) zu hieven – und trifft auf Joan v. Ehren: eine Engländerin, die in Deutschland's hohem Norden, in Hamburg, zur Preußin wurde – nicht von Geburt, aber doch wohl nach göttlicher Planung (vermutet Joan) und – wichtiger – nach innerer Einstellung und Haltung.

YES – dieses Wort in seiner ursprünglichen Bedeutung ist ihr ebenso zum Lebensmotto geworden wie auch die Umdeutung in

YES! – YOUR ENGLISH SERVICES

Joan's English Training ist viel mehr als nur eine Sprachen-Schule: Es ist eine Fan-Gemeinde, über viele Jahre verbunden durch die regelmäßig erschienenen Ausgaben von TRAINFO – einer Mischung von Beiträgen zu aktuellen politischen oder auch skurrilen Themen (der Übergang ist hier fließend!); Grammatik und Sprachkunde werden mit viel Humor geboten. Vor allem aber ist TRAINFO ein Kaleidoskop ganz persönlicher Gedanken von Joan v. Ehren.

Hier schreibt eine Autorin „aus der Seele (ihrer eigenen) für die Seele (ihrer Leser)" vor dem Hintergrund eines Lebensweges, dem manche Höhen vergönnt waren, der aber nicht zuletzt auch etliche Hürden, ja große Barrieren überwinden mußte.

Außerordentliche Lebenserfahrungen prägen ein außerordentliches Profil: Joan v. Ehren, Ms.-Managerin, gestattet uns – unplugged – mit den folgenden Beiträgen, ausgesucht aus vielen Trainfo-Artikeln, einen Blick in die Feinheiten Ihres Profils. Und so wird dann plötzlich – mit einem kleinen Augenzwinkern – aus dem scheinbar chaotischen „Joan's Jungle" ein preußisches Lebensbild.

Dr. Jürgen Bruns

Dr. Jürgen Bruns ist Vorsitzender des Vorstandes der Europa Carton AG, einem der führenden Verpackungsmittelhersteller in Deutschland und dem Unternehmen YES! über viele Jahre freundschaftlich verbunden.

JOAN THE GERMOPHILE

'Joan the Germophile', that's me! At least, after over 30 years in Germany I have to admit that I have been won over by their correctness (no, it's not pedantry), their self-assurance (no, it's not arrogance), their seriousness (no, it's not unfriendliness) and – yes – their sense of humour!

Of course, I am fortunate that most of my contacts to Germans are within the parameters of my various passions: management, banking, marketing, IT, horses, dogs and teaching English (plus my secret love of golf). This means that I can delight in their acribic exactitude which provides a benchmark for my own efforts.

Gone are the days when I could nonchalantly put off until tomorrow what should be done today. Gone too are the days of take-it-easy, relaxed bonhomie, that heart-warming trait of the English which enables them to patiently endure the inefficiencies of their daily life.

I have become a hard-working, hard-hitting, say-it-like-it-is Teutonian. And I'm proud of the fact – even if I am no longer as popular with my friends as I once was. Certainly not now that I preface most remarks with: "We in Germany do things differently to you here in England!" No prospect then of returning to Merry Old England when my working days are over – I would feel like a fish out of water, in spite of the agreeable friendliness, the endless cups of tea and orderly queues. If there is such a phenomenon as predestination, I think God actually intended me to be a German (preferably a Bavarian – another secret passion of mine) but got confused on the day I was born and had the stork take the wrong turning and drop me in England, instead.

Certainly the first 'love of my life' was a boy called Michael Kellner from Düsseldorf, who came to my home town on an exchange visit when he was fourteen and I was thirteen. When I told him that I already had a boyfriend (I started young!) he prophetically replied: "The German oak will conquer the English grass."

The only aspect of life in Germany that worries me is that the high standards which have impressed me over the years seem to be slipping, and "things ain't what they used to be", as the song says. I was encouraged, therefore, to make the acquaintance recently of a delightful gentleman in his early sixties – a Prussian through and through – who epitomised all that I had believed the Germans to be. So, in my next life I think I will ask God to send me back to earth as a 'bayerischer Preiß'!

GERMLISH

After so many years of living in Germany and listening to Germans speaking English, it is not surprising that I am sometimes mistaken for a German when I am in England. Every now and then I say something and think: "Is that English or German?" If the other person looks bewildered, it is usually German.

Then there is the problem of "Germanisms" – you know, a direct translation from German into English in traditional "Lübke"-style. One of my best was when I said: "I'll go into town to foot!" "To foot?" said my mother, who doesn't know the German. "To foot? Don't you mean 'on foot'? And you are supposed to be an English teacher!"

On my annual visit to England, strangers usually ask me: "You're not English, are you? Where are you from?"
"Hamburg"
"Really? Well, your English is excellent!"
"Thank you," I say (God forgive me!)
It is not only these occasional mistakes which make people think that I am a German tourist. There are other problems which I face when returning to my home country. For example, the money system changed just before I came to Germany, and I still can never quite

work out which are the 1p, 2p, 5p and 20p coins. Usually the shop assistant takes pity on me and sorts out my money for me, whereupon I say, "Sank you werry much!" in my best German accent!

I'll never forget the time in Harrods when, for once, I checked my change (I normally never do because I can't count to save my life!) However, on this occasion we were in the Harrods "pub". I had given the barkeeper a 5 pound note for two beers and he only gave me a few coins change. I knew that even Harrod's beer couldn't be that expensive. So I said in my most polite and subservient voice, "Could you check my change, please?" And the barkeeper rapidly counted it out – up to 5 pounds.

"But where are the pounds?", I asked.

"These are pounds, madam!" he said in his best arrogant "Harrods" manner, pointing to some small coins. (I didn't know that the pound coin had been introduced since my last visit).

"Sank you werry much, but in Chermany ve do not haff zis money", I explained.

Then there was the time when I momentarily forgot which side of the road I was driving on, and turned right – on the "wrong" side – and suddenly found myself facing three lanes of traffic. I immediately realized my mistake as there was no fanfare of carhorns as there would have been in Germany! All the cars waited patiently while I manoeuvred myself out of trouble. One driver wound his window down,

"You must be a foreigner!"

"Er .. um ... er ... um ... er .. yes"

"Have a nice holiday!"

"Sank you werry much!"

AW' ROI', DUCK!

One of the first problems which face the conscientious Germans visiting Great Britain or America is to understand what the native speaker is saying. It doesn't matter how good your English is, or how much time and money you have spent in perfecting it, if you can't understand the other person, you are lost!

Just how lost you could be, became clear to me on my last visit to England. The flight would have been easy for you, a toffee-nosed stewardess with her mouth full of hot potatoes was up-staging even the Queen! "The aaeerrooplaayyne willll beeee laaaynding in djust aaya mohment".

The problems started after landing. I was standing at the bus stop, wondering if the next bus was going to be punctual when a smart woman in airbus uniform came up to me, and said in broad cockney:

" 'Allo, luv. You wai'in' for the airbus?"

"Yes", I said. "But last time I had to wait nearly an hour. They filled up at Terminal 1 and didn't come here to Terminal 2."

"Yeah, it's a roi' mess. They fill up an' just scarper off up the mo'erway to Lon'on! I' ain' 'arf embarrassin'!"

Two problems – one of slang and one of dialect – the Londoners typically swallow their "t's", "g's" and "h's", giving a glottal stop instead.

Northerners, on the other hand, swallow the frequent word "the", say "t'book", as in "Gimme t'book, willya, duck". The Midlanders have a harder accent: "Coom on, Marlene, gerra move on, willya!"

Of course, we all have problems in America! I will let you into a secret: it's not just Germans who can't understand them – I am completely lost, too. In fact, when I was in a New York shop last year, I had to plead with the sales assistant: "Look, I'm a foreigner from England – I can't understand a word you're saying! So please speak slowly and clearly – and use words of one syllable!" He looked at me rather pityingly, but as he wanted to make the sale, he tried to slow down.

So, what is the solution? If it's dialect, just smile sweetly, nod and shake your head at a ratio of 3:1 and they will think you are a very intelligent, charming person!

HI, BILL! GREAT TO SEE YOU!

After living in Germany for over half my life, I have possibly become even more German than the Germans. At least, when one of my German colleagues criticised me for being 'more pedantic than the worst of the Prussians', I took it as a compliment.

This metamorphosis has taken on different forms, one of them being the acquired preference for the more formal types of address, a reluctance to use 'du' and a greater ease with the use of surnames rather than first names.

Such formal parameters are a useful tool; they make it easier to have an 'eyeball to eyeball and see who shoots first' showdown; and they mean that it is possible to show a greater affection for a business partner than might be possible if one were on first name terms.

All this, of course, is in direct contrast to the customs in England and America where first names are used in almost all situations. This use of the first name in no way implies friendship or familiarity. Quite the opposite, it could well be a smokescreen to hide the forthcoming assassination attempt: "Hi, Bill! How are you? Great to see you!" And WOOMPF – there is Bill, lying on the ground in a pool of blood with a knife in his back (figuratively speaking, that is).

It is only usual to use surnames if the other person is at least a generation older than yourself, in which case they will call you by your first name and you will say Mr. or Mrs So-and-so to them. Anyone in a position of authority, such as a teacher or a doctor of medicine, will also be formally addressed, using their title if they have one.

Two worlds – two customs. And I, as neither a true German nor a true Englishwoman, but rather a mongrel combination of both, live in a schizophrenic limbo-land. I am 'Joan' to my friends (particularly horsy and doggy ones) 'Joan' on cassettes, 'Joan v. E.' in quasi formal correspondence – but woe betide anyone in business who calls me 'Joan' to my face, if I always address them by their surnames and their title.

Which brings me to another point – can anyone tell me how to overcome that in-between stage when affection and friendship have reached a point where it is ridiculous to continue using surnames and titles, but etiquette precludes the use of first names, so that you end up by using no names at all?

DOG WAGS TAIL AT CAT

Intercultural awareness is the buzz word of the moment. No longer is it just a question of learning another language with its grammar, vocabulary and idioms. It is even more important to be aware of the differences between cultures. Just transferring a phrase directly from one language to the other is often not sufficient, even if the sentence is grammatically correct. The same expression may not have the same meaning in both cultures. After all, if two animals wag their tails this is fine if they are both dogs – but not if one is a dog and the other is a cat!

For this reason, intercultural questions of etiquette are becoming increasingly significant, particularly such seemingly unimportant aspects as to which name to use, greetings, introductions and other polite expressions.

People coming from English-speaking countries, such as Australia, New Zealand, South African, Canada – not to mention the UK and the USA – all have the same tradition of using first names and have to adjust quickly to the German habit of using surnames for all but the closest of friends. A colleague of mine, a trainer from Australia who worked for three years with Arthur Andersen in Perth after majoring in accounting and business law, and who then went on to work for four years as a consultant to investment banks in London, says: "In all seven years of my business life I have never been called by my surname, nor have I called anyone by their surnames – not even the biggest bosses."

Germans, of course, find it unusual to be on first-name terms right from the start with someone they don't know. The problem is made more complicated by the fact that one is sometimes conversing with foreigners for whom English is only their third language, and who have a completely different cultural background, for example people from Sweden, Asia or Eastern Europe. In addition, non-Germans who have spent many years in Germany have often become more German than the Germans, which adds to the confusion!

Of course, one solution could be not to use any names at all! This is certainly an emergency solution if you have a temporary blackout and can't remember the person's name. However, whatever the customs, one thing is certain – using a person's name builds a personal bridge beyond that person's function or status to the individual. "I am Joan!" – not an just an anonymous English trainer or a businesswoman, an interchangeable no-name commodity.

My advice is to react, rather than act in situations where you are uncertain about the correct form. Introduce yourself by using both first name and surname (this is usual in English, we never just use the surname, as is typical in Germany) and see which name the other person picks up. For example, I often introduce myself by saying: "I'm Joan – Joan von Ehren". By repeating the first name, I am signaling that this is the name I want to be used (in the same way as James Bond always says: "Bond. James Bond.")

The other person, if a native speaker, will usually respond by saying: "Pleased to meet you, Joan. I'm Mike, Mike Richardson."Then, of course, I reply with: "Pleased to meet you too, Mike." – or some similar greeting. If someone persists in saying "Mrs von Ehren", I say: "Do call me Joan!", as I really do dislike being called by my surname when speaking English. Not only is it untypical, but – worst still, in England only very old ladies are referred to by their surnames (!)

And it certainly is an absolute "no-no" to use somebody's surname if they have just called you by your first name! It is a really harsh rebuff, and means that you are saying: "Who are you, little nobody, to call ME by my first name! Don't you know who I am? Please treat me with more respect in future!!"

It is important to remember that we do not have the "Du" and "Sie" mechanism in English. We have different instruments to draw people closer towards us or push them away. And using the first name is normal and natural, and most certainly not the equivalent of "duzen" in German.

My final advice on this whole issue of intercultural awareness is to make it a topic of conversation, and ask the other person about traditions in their country. This indicates a cosmopolitan interest in other nationalities, showing that you are aware of intercultural differences and want to learn about other customs.

YOU CAN SAY "YOU" TO ME

When I first came to Germany I had huge problems in deciding whether to say "Du" or "Sie". (Have you ever thought about the fact that Germans say "Sie" to acquaintances and "Du" to friends – unless they sleep with them, in which case they become acquaintances again, as in: "Ich möchte Ihnen meinen Bekannten vorstellen".) In English-speaking countries it is much easier because there is only the one form of address: "you". Nevertheless there are still some points to note, as it is not always as simple as it appears at first sight:

First of all, it is important to realize that, although the British and Americans normally use first names and "you", this does not have the familiarity of the German "duzen". Its nearest equivalent in German is probably first names and "Sie".

If we want to become more friendly with a person we do this via a series of invitations from: "Shall we go out for a drink?"; "Would you like to go out for dinner this evening?" – to the more friendly: "Would you like to come round for supper this evening?"

Only when a series of private invitations have been given, is the real offer of friendship signaled: "Drop in any time." Opening up one's home for spontaneous visits – usually to have a cup of tea – is the equivalent to the German "du", and takes just as long to develop.

The Germans use the instrument of "Du/Sie" in order to create the necessary respect. We have different signals – body language or the tone of voice – in order to show someone very clearly if they are being over familiar. After all, as the traditional class society, the British are masters at keeping people in their place!

As such social customs take a life-time to learn, my advice to you would be to take your signals from the way in which people introduce themselves to you. If they give you their first names, use yours as well. If they use their surnames, then the situation is extremely formal and you should use your surname too.

In this case, it is usual to shake hands and reply to their: "How do you do?" by repeating "How do you do?" This is only said at the first meeting, and is usually followed by: "Pleased to meet you!", with the reply: "Pleased to meet you, too!" After this initial introduction, the usual greeting is "How are you?" to which the answer is "Fine, thanks. And you?"

Don't shake hands, bow, click your heels or even – horror of continental horrors – kiss their hands and/or cheeks! Or make the mistake of thinking that the businessman who has just given you his first name is your friend – he has probably got a knife hidden behind his back waiting to stick it into you at the first opportunity!

When I first came to Germany one of my biggest problems was to know which form of greeting to use. I was told that I had to say "Sie" to all people older than myself, and "Du" to those younger.

Now this is not as easy as it sounds! How do you know how old people are? It's not so bad if they are obviously ancient – but this was in the 60's when German young people hadn't yet woken up to the delights of the mini-skirt and swinging Carnaby Street. A lot of young girls looked quite mature, and if I decided to play it safe and say, "Sie", they often said, "You can say, 'Du' to me, I am only thirteen"!

My books on German etiquette gave me tips on when I could offer someone my "Du" and when I had to wait for them to offer theirs to me. Apparently, as a lady (was I one?) I could offer a gentleman my "Du", unless his rank and wealth put him so far above me that I had to wait for him to offer his "Du" to me. On the other hand, I had to wait for another lady to offer me her "Du". especially if she was older.

And then there was the problem of the "Bruderkuß" – from whom could I expect a passionate kiss, and from whom would I just get a limp handshake? I found out that, true to Murphy's Law, the more attractive they were, the less likely I was to get a kiss – there was usually some female guard nearby!

Oh yes, these handshakes! I soon realized that I must shake hands all the time – when I came and when I left. In fact, at parties I never had time to enjoy myself. By the time I had gone around shaking everybody's hand, working out how old or rich they were to see if I could give them my "Du", waiting expectantly for sloppy kisses from the only attractive man there, it was time to say goodbye, and go round shaking hands again!

Now I am so Germanised that it is quite embarrassing when I am in England. My hand shoots out all the time like a cowboy with his six-gun, and English people who don't know this German custom just look at my outstretched hand in bewilderment.

Don't think that life has got any easier after 25 years' practice! It's even more complicated now that I'm a "gruftie". If the person is younger, and I say, "You can say 'Du' to me", they are usually so embarrassed that they either continue to say "Sie", or don't say another word! With older people life is more difficult still. I have to compare wrinkles , count gray hairs and get out my pocket calculator to compute the results until I know which of us can take this important step.

In England? It's easy! You can say "you" to everybody!

WHO'S SPEAKING, PLEASE?

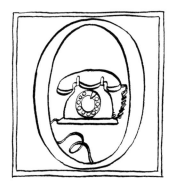

One major aspect of intercultural communication is the differences in customs and habits between different countries. Behavioural patterns that are acceptable in one society appear extremely impolite in the other.

Take, for example, the telephone. It is perfectly usual for the English person to answer the phone either by giving the telephone number or by saying, "Hallo!" – and nothing else. To the Germans, this seems to be very rude. They think that the English person is either unwilling or unable to give his or her name. Not at all! It is just not usual to answer the phone as the Germans do, by giving one's name – as well as the name of the firm.

Mind you, most Germans usually speak so fast that it all sounds like Double-Dutch – and one is no wiser at the end. In fact, some people usually gabble on for such a long time, that I often wonder whether or not they are also giving me such intimate details as the number of their lovers, their date of birth – or the number of corns on their big toes! Of course, as I can't understand them, it doesn't matter. Except, of course, for the telephone bill. Just think of all those millions of DM you could save yearly if people just said "hallo", instead of giving you their CV.

Or perhaps not. After all, it takes just as long to pry the speaker's name out of him, if you are calling an English firm. Some people are so reluctant to tell you anything that you would think that they are hiding a bank robber.

So, next time you call England or an English company in Germany, don't be frustrated, just ask: "Who's speaking, please?" – and you never know, you might be in for a wonderful surprise as the answer could be "ME"!

DON'T INTERRUPT!

Did you know that Germans are chronic interrupters? You don't believe me? Just watch what happens next time you are talking to somebody in a public place. If you are seen by someone you know, they will probably walk up to you and immediately start talking. "Hallo, Joan. Have you heard the latest news about …?"

The person you were talking to will not even look worried. He or she will either just wait patiently until the interruption is over. Or will walk away to look for a conversation which they can interrupt.

You still don't believe me? Watch what happens next time the telephone rings when you are visiting somebody. Your conversation partner will not say: "I'm sorry, but I have a visitor. Could I ring you back?"

They will talk and talk and talk and talk, and leave you counting the paper clips on the desk or the flowers on the wallpaper. In fact, they will even go into the most intimate details about their personal or business life. Exactly as if you were not there.

And what do you do? You sit there patiently and politely waiting for the call to end. Then you take a deep breath and carry on from where you left off as if nothing had happened! This can go on indefinitely! I have had business appointments when the phone has rung literally every five minutes, leaving me in mid-sentence, mouth open like a stranded goldfish!

Of course, the polite English way isn't much good either. It is considered very rude to interrupt an ongoing conversation. So the potential interrupter will stand as close as he can to the people in conversation without actually treading on their toes. Then he will try to attract their attention by coughing, jumping up and down as if he were in urgent need of the toilet, raising his hand – maybe even snapping his fingers.

This will go on for some hours, or as long as it takes for the conversation to finish. Then, and only then can he say: "Hallo, Joan (as if he had just walked up). Have you heard the latest news about …?"

So, what is the solution? If the matter is urgent and time is short, you can say: "Excuse me, may I interrupt for a moment?" Then say what you have to say, as quickly and briefly as you can. And escape immediately before you are recognized!

SMILE PLEASE...

I was talking to an air hostess the other day, and I asked her if she liked her job. "If it wasn't for the fact that the German passengers are so rude, it would be a good life. Someone should really teach them to say 'please' and 'thank you'!"

At a seminar I once attended, the English lecturer said, "I have one major request to make to you teachers of 'English as a Foreign Language' – please teach your German students how to be polite. They so often offend their English hosts with their rudeness!"

These two incidents illustrate one of the problems of speaking in a foreign language. It is not just a question of correct grammar, but of expression, as well as body language and a relaxed interest in the other person.

Germans, in particular, want to be perfect, and are therefore so often tense and worried about making mistakes. This can make them appear far more unfriendly than they really are. Instead of their usual smile, they look "grimmig" and "verbissen". In their concentration, they fold their arms, frown and stare at the ceiling – all signals of reserve and rejection.

Then, of course, there are expressions which are perfectly acceptable in one language, but which are extremely impolite in another. In German, you can say: "Bringen Sie mir ein Bier." This sounds TERRIBLE in English! We would say: "May I have a beer, please?" which sounds really "DOOF" in German!

Sometimes the speaker is so relieved at having been able to understand the question and formulate an answer, that they forget the basic rules of politeness – to ask the other person about themselves. The little question: "And what about you?" is magic and will open many conversational doors.

My advice to all German speakers of English is: "Don't worry, be happy!" I am a "Germophile" – or whatever the equivalent to "Anglophile" or "Francophile" is. I love Germans – I've married two, so I must do! So, when you speak English, just take a deep breath, relax, smile, forget about making mistakes – and enjoy the conversation!

…AND HE DID!

Ha! I have won a great victory and am extremely proud of myself! No, I haven't closed a million-dollar deal. And I haven't driven the competition to bankruptcy. Nothing financial – I have proved that friendliness can win out in the end!

Every time I come back from either America or England,

I am faced with these grumpy-looking, dour-faced, non-smiling, bad-tempered passport control officials at Fuhlsbüttel, Hamburg's airport.

Of course, they fit in with the general ambiance of the airport which doesn't exactly hit you in the eye with its friendly atmosphere (particularly since you now have to pay DM 2.50 – and only get 50 pfennigs back – if you want to use a luggage trolley, and who has that sort of small change when flying in from abroad???).

Well, when I flew back from England recently I decided to do something about the situation. I got in the queue in front of a particularly glum-looking passport controller, and started to psyche him out mentally. I fixed my eye and focused my mind, willing him to to his knees.

When it was finally my turn, the corners of his mouth turned down even further when he looked at my passport photo (which admittedly makes me look like a cross between a drunk RAF terrorist and my own grandmother). Then he glared at me fiercely as if he expected me to pull out a gun any moment and shoot him.

Now came my big moment. I turned on my sweetest smile: "Guten Abend". Nix da 'guten Abend' – at least, he didn't move a muscle! But I blew his mind! I bent forward, smiled even more sweetly and said (in English) : "You could smile, you know. It really won't hurt you!" And what do you know, his face broke into the broadest smile and he shouted with laughter!

Which all goes to prove that passport controllers have got a heart somewhere under all that uniform – and a sense of humour. What a pity they don't show it more often!

SERVICE GERMAN-STYLE

A recent Newsweek title story was entitled: The Germans do not know the meaning of the word 'Service'. It related the experiences of a Newsweek correspondent who has been living in Germany for some years.

We, Brits and Yanks, who are used to a more obvious friendliness, are tempted to agree. Even a German, having recently returned from America, complained about the cold, unfriendly atmosphere back here in Hamburg. He hadn't noticed it before, but it hit him in the eye after he had had the chance to compare the two cultures.

What is the truth? Having lived here for over thirty years, and now being more German than English, I don't like to hear my beloved Germans criticised. Yet, when I see the unsmiling faces of sales assistants, the bored expressions of cashiers, the arrogant glance of waiters and the pigheadedness of civil servants, I am inclined to agree. Certainly, it is no wonder that the impression given to strangers is one of belligerence and gloominess.

But there is another side to this story. My experience with dour Teutonians is that they love to laugh, they greatly appreciate humour and open up to friendliness like flowers in the desert when it rains!

I have discovered that it is wrong to wait for the other person to smile – they often can't, at least not as a first move.

No, I smile first! If they have a name tag, I look at it and address them by name. "Mr. So-and-so, I need expert advice, and I am sure you can help me!" You should see the look on Mr. So-and-so's face! He lights up like a beacon and is prepared to tear out an arm and a leg to give me the best service possible.

If I am telephoning with an unknown person, an anonymous cog in the wheel of a huge organisation, like Telecom, I ask them for their name, and I use it. Again, my request for their assistance and my assurance that I know they can help, works miracles. Like conspirators, they don't let up until they have found the solution for me. And we end up feeling like blood brothers.

It works! Really! I have allies and buddies among civil servants, police officers (who regularly catch me driving where I shouldn't, and wave me on with a smile!), waiters, shop assistants, doctors, dentists, craftsmen, car park assistants – and best of all – with bankers!

Mind you, I have one secret weapon! If I meet someone who refuses to melt at my friendliness (and the exception proves the rule) I hit back with all the unfriendliness, arrogance and aggression that I have learnt through living 30 years in merry old Germany!

PS: No, there is one situation where even I can't find anything to praise about my adopted compatriots. Put a German behind the steering wheel of a big car and he/she turns into a rabid panther! And no, I don't respond with friendliness, but with a very rude word!

FOUR-LETTER WORDS

In one of my English lessons, we were discussing the problem of marriages where one partner is at least twenty years older than the other, and whether it is more problematic if the woman is older than the man. "Of course there are more problems," said someone. "If the woman is younger, she can service the man, but if she is older she has to service herself."

I immediately collapsed with laughter.
"What's the matter? I only meant that she can bring him his meals when he is ill"

"Then you mean 'serve', not 'service'! 'Service' is what women do to men in Thai brothels!"

Of course, I couldn't resist telling my colleagues about this beautiful mistake. "I have the same problem in one of my groups", said Jacky. "One of them is a do-it-yourself man, and he asked me what he could say for 'basteln' as in: 'I like to go to my cellar and 'basteln'. I can't say 'I like to go into my cellar and do-it-myself!"
"Well, you could use the word 'tinker'!", I suggested.

"I can't say that!" laughed Jacky. "Shall I tell him to say, 'My hobby is to go into my cellar and have a tinker'!"

We tried for several minutes to find some expression which did not have a sexual double meaning, but gave it up as hopeless. That is one of the problems of the puritan English heritage. Nobody likes to talk about sex directly, everything has to be wrapped up in innuendos. This can give almost everything a double meaning.

The Americans are more down-to-earth and come straight out with f*** and sh** and other crude expressions. The English disguise such swear words: f***ing is 'flipping', 'hell' is 'heck', 'God' is 'gosh', 'Jesus Christ' is 'jeepers creepers'.

I was brought up not to swear, and even today try not to use any strong swear words. On the other hand, I find myself quite easily saying 'Scheiße' in German, because in my ears it doesn't sound as bad as 'shit' But I have frequently been told not to use this word as it is not fitting for an 'English lady'!

I would like to pass this warning on to you. Even if you know English swear words, don't use them! As a non-native speaker, one doesn't have the finer feeling to know when and how to use them properly – and it can sound really crude and primitive if used wrongly.

FLINGING AND FLIRTING

One of the nicest things about the otherwise wasted time at the hairdresser's is that it is a great chance to read all the magazines which give 'invaluable' advice on make-up, beauty, fashion and life-style. Of course, I always pretend to be above such trash, but, like every woman, cannot resist the temptation to devour this information whenever I get the chance. (It's like nobody admits to reading 'Bildzeitung' or eating 'Big Macs' – but their turnovers are astronomical!)

Anyway, on my last visit I was interested to read an article in Cosmopolitan on 'flingen' and 'flirten'. (Whoever creates these Germanized versions of English slang? And what is their conjugation: flingen, flang, geflungen and flirten, flitt, geflitten???)

Apparently, 'flirten' is the same in mega-straight Germany as is 'to flirt' in I-love-my-hot-water-bottle England. It is the almost forgotten art of sending "you-are-the-most-fascinating-person-I-have-ever-met" signals to the opposite sex. If the other person is also a master of the art of flirtation, the mutual back-patting, ego-boosting ball can be thrown back and forth for as long as the buzz lasts. This sophisticated communication ends as it began, with no further consequences than that both ball-players leave each other, walking on air and feeling like a million dollars.

'Flingen', comes from the English 'to have a fling' and means to let the flirtation lead to its natural biological conclusion, also with no further consequences – unless one neglects the warnings of the health authorities.

The advice of Cosmopolitan to the modern single woman, therefore, is not to regard each chance meeting with an unattached man as an opportunity to get married, but to just enjoy the chemical interaction between the sexes.

This openness, say the experts, is the secret of the mystique of sex-appeal. It is not a question of looks alone, but the ability to make the other person feel that they – and you – are desirable and unique.

Hey, that sounds like a good recipe for soft selling! I'll have to try it out! "What do you want to buy, Joan or an English course?" No, on second thoughts, I think I prefer staying at home and reading the 'Handelsblatt'!

SEX APPEAL

I was amused by a recent article in 'Hör Zu' entitled: "What women find sexy about men!" I thought this was a nice twist, as we poor women are always getting brainwashed about having to be blonde, blue-eyed, bosomy and beautiful (intelligence is definitely a no-no!) if we want to attract a man!

So, what were the conclusions? Brawny muscles, perfect looks, tall, dark and handsome? Surprisingly, no! Perfect looks and a perfect body are, apparently, not important, and the Greek gods in perfume adverts are a total turn-off.

Over 50% of the women interviewed said that a man's butt was what turned them on the most. Others chose such characteristics as humour and being a good listener.

One woman looked first at a man's hands, another preferred sexy movements (I always thought such men were gay!) For a third woman, it was power, success and big cars (like the ugly little man, always accompanied by the most beautiful women, who said: "The secret of my sex appeal is on my bank account!")

A Burt Reynolds chest (a controversial point: Andrew Agassi shaved his chest to please Barbara Streisand; others buy a wig for their chest to prove their manliness!) Sexy underclothes (black lace jock-straps and tiger tanga?) A seductive glance, suggestive gestures and broad shoulders. Small imperfections like a gap between the teeth, a scar in the face, untidy hair.

Marie-Luise Marjan chose Donald Sutherland, saying that he has a flair which is secretive, intelligent and curious. For Claudia Schiffer, eyes and voice are erotic characteristics.

I can relate to that! I know a guy who has such a Pavarotti voice that he only needs to say "Hi!" and I get the mega-flash of the century! Yeah! Believe it or not, even Cowboy Joan has very clear ideas on what is sexy and what isn't – she's just not telling!

LONELY HEARTS

At present I am 'between men' – and am really enjoying this sabbatical leave! However my contentment with my present state-of-the-nation does not stop me from appraising the 'market' both at home and abroad. For this reason I take particular note of the occasional 'lonely hearts' advertisements in, would you believe it, the Handelsblatt! One requirement common to these elite swains is a desire for a woman who is not only young, beautiful, rich, intelligent, well-born and well-bred but who is also, and I quote: "Parkettsicher".

When I first read this expression, my favourite little devil whispered in my ear: "Does that mean she has to be able to do it on the dance floor?" But as that particular lonely heart was a Swiss Bankier, I can only presume that was not what he meant!

No, I think it means that the lady in question knows not to pick her nose, spit, make rude noises or clean her ears when she is at the Viennese Opera Ball. And presumably knows which title to use and when to use it (never call an Englishman "doctor" unless he's a medicus), when to be arrogant, when to be subservient, when to curtsey and when to offer a limp hand to be 'kissed'.

By the time I had reached this conclusion, all my little devils were gathered around me, whispering and chattering in anxious fear, poking and prodding me, pleading with me never to try and meet this standard because it would make them jobless. "No, you needn't worry," I comforted them. "Parkettsicher is BORING!"

Which means, of course, that the next man in my life will not be a Swiss Bankier, but as I am not young, beautiful, rich, intelligent, well-born and well-bred, I wouldn't have had a chance, anyway!

POTATOES AND SOUP SPOONS

This whole question of being 'parkettsicher' really has me worried. After all, if we take this to mean mastering correct etiquette at all times, we end up with an insolvable problem – what sort of etiquette are we talking about? Let me show you what I mean. When I first came to Germany 30 years ago, I thought I was a relatively well-brought-up English girl. Nix da! When, as is usual in England, I cut my potatoes with a knife, I was deafened with screams of horror from my future sister-in-law. In Germany, cutting your potatoes with a knife is apparently SHOCKING!!

Of course, as a mannerly Englishwoman I – as is only polite – said nothing about my mannerless sister-in-law who shoveled her food onto the front of her fork instead of pressing it daintily onto the back (yes, even peas!!); who ate her soup from the tip of the spoon instead of tilting it sideways; and who tipped the soup plate towards, instead of away from, the edge of the table.

And what about these German men? It is no wonder that they have an international reputation for rudeness when, in a restaurant, they charge ahead of their accompanying lady leaving her to follow. Hasn't every English lady learnt from childhood to judge a man's class by his ability to let her go first on all occasions. Are not the contortions which are required to keep the umbrella over her head to protect her from the perpetual English rain, open the door of the restaurant, let her pass, close the umbrella, enter himself without slamming the door, take her coat, remove his own, indicate the direction she should take towards the table he has reserved, draw out her chair for her, gently push it forward without banging her heels (and that all from the rear) – I repeat, are not these contortions evidence of class, breeding and possibly even the promise of talent in other areas?

Imagine my startled surprise recently when a man, who should have known better, accompanied me on a short walk through town on the inside of the pavement when every English gentleman knows that his place is always, but always, on the kerbside – to protect the lady's robes from being splashed by passing vehicles. When I tactfully mentioned this fact, my companion was not the least abashed, but murmured something about having to walk on my left to protect me with his sword!

Indeed it would seem to be only the dance floor where there is international agreement: the man has to lead – small comfort for me who learnt to dance at my all-girls school, where, being the tallest girl, I always had to be the 'man'. Which means that, even today, if I am not concentrating I can still commit that most unforgivable of sins – and make the man go where Joan wants!!!!

LUCKY MEN

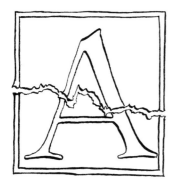Apparently I am better at separating from my husbands than living with them. At least, the present score of two ex-husbands who are now going around with very relieved expressions on their faces would seem to confirm this! In fact, my first husband presented me with 20 red roses for 'twenty (for him) happy years of marriage' on the occasion of our divorce, and I invited him out for a lobster and champagne dinner to celebrate my new-found freedom.

My second husband and I also parted in amicable harmony. The advantage of this arrangement for him is that he is now free to look for a more housewifely partner than career-minded, workaholic Joan could be. And I am free to work as long as is required, read the 'Handelsblatt' in bed, watch ntv instead of sport and turn up my 'Pavarotti and Friends' record as loudly as I want!

The necessity (for me) for this arrangement lies in the disparity between career men and career women: A successful career man will traditionally come home to his loving wife whose job it is to do all things necessary for his comfort. He can sit down with his newspaper, a glass of wine and put his feet up to wait for dinner.

Business guests will be entertained, wined and dined at his expense, but not at his effort. Seasonal festivities can be enjoyed in a relaxed manner, as the goose has been cooked, the presents purchased and wrapped, and sufficient food bought in to fill all the hungry mouths.

If he has to go on a business trip, his clothes will be washed, ironed and ready-waiting in his over-night traveller. He can rush from the office to go straight on holiday, because the family luggage will be packed, arrangements made for the cats, dogs and plants, the fridge defrosted and the water turned off.

Not so for the career woman unless she has the luxury of a houseman to care for her creature comforts (but he would probably be a mindless toy-boy who would bore her to death!). If she, too, is married to a successful business man she will have the double burden of pursuing her profession, yet creating a home where both feel comfortable and at ease.

Well, I've played both roles for 30 years, and now that I have established my dynasty and can pride myself on my position as family matriach I have decided that enough is enough. What I need now is an APRIL: an Almost Perfect Romantic Intelligent Lover with a wife or live-in partner at home to do the work and leave me to enjoy the fun bits!

SINGLE SATISFACTION

Being partnerless for the first time since I was thirteen is an exciting experience. One of the more challenging aspects of life as a swinging single is the necessity of going places alone. Used to always having a male companion, it was quite strange at first to go to a restaurant, a concert or the theatre on my own. Sure, I can always ask one of my women friends to accompany me – and sometimes I am even bold enough to invite a man (wow!). But true independence presupposes the freedom to go solo.

Maybe a woman's innate reluctance to go out alone has to do with her desire for male protection. Certainly, it is not easy. Nevertheless, once I had taken the plunge I became quite addicted to my own company. Certainly, this year's holiday, which I spent alone, was one of the best I have ever had. And I no longer even bat an eyelid when I go out for a meal with myself!

At least, then, there is no problem with who samples the wine! I am always amused by the uncertainty that many waiters show when it is clear to them that it is the woman who has invited the man. Although it is usually the man who is expected to test the wine for temperature and cork, I was pleasantly surprised recently when dining out in one of the better restaurants in Hamburg, that the waiter quite matter-of-factly poured the wine into my glass! And tactfully, he immediately responded to my "do you think?" gesture, and gave my guest the wine to taste, too. So we were both happy!

Strange as it may seem, however, even an old grandmother like myself has to deal with bothersome guys who think that going solo is a state that has to be remedied – and preferably by them! Annoying as such overtures are, I can live with them. And I am certainly not going to allow these Romeos to intimidate me into staying at home. Quite the opposite, I have developed a perfect 'Queen-Mother, look-down-my-nose, freeze-you-to-death' arrogance which makes them retreat fast and leave me in peace to enjoy my own company!

I NEED A MAN!

"I need a man!" This exclamation has passed my lips more than once since becoming a swinging single. Not for the reasons you may think! No, not even Big Joan would go around shouting out her erotic desires! It is far more basic than that:

Just take the problem of parking. Men have an inbuilt, inborn parking device – just watch little boys playing "Brumm! Brumm!" with their toy cars and you'll see what I mean. Men can get into and out of the tightest parking spaces. Women can't. Or perhaps I should say, I can't. I need six feet of space all around my car before I can even think of manoeuvring. I can't get in – or once in, I can't get out.

But no way do I make the mistake of trying to park or de-park the car myself. No! Immediately I see that the neighbouring car is dangerously close to mine, I get out, approach the most attractive man I can find with a sweet smile and say: "I need a man!" (Actually, it works better in English than in German.)

My victim's eyes light up in anticipation – and only show a brief flash of disappointment when he realises that I only want him for my car. After all, the chance of playing "Brumm! Brumm!" in the presence of an admiring (and helpless) woman is too good to be missed!

Ditto when my battery is flat! In this case, it is not as if I am completely helpless. At least, I know the name of those funny cables which connect battery to battery. They are called 'jump leads'. But that is sufficient, thank you very much! "I need a man" to jump start my car. And it is more much exciting to watch him doing it than to get oil on my manicured nails.

You see, there are things in life a woman just should not learn (if she does, she will find herself having to do them all the time.) After all, is it feminine to drill holes in walls, wallpaper rooms, paint doors or sandpaper radiators? Should I get ugly muscles by lifting heavy things or carrying crates of drinks? And doesn't the wine taste so much better if a man opens the bottle (unless I am on my own, in which case I can open the bottle very well myself!)

Feminists have made life more difficult for themselves. Personally, I only support emancipation if it means that I can get my own way and do my own thing. Otherwise, I am an old-fashioned woman who likes a man to be a man, and do all the manly things only men can do – like hunting buffalo and killing tigers, protecting me from highwaymen and finding gold mines!

WRONG! I NEED A WOMAN!

OK, so the cry of my heart is: I need a man! Wrong! Now Christmas time is drawing near, it's not a man I need, but a woman! A woman to decorate my flat and trim the tree. To buy presents and wrap them prettily. To make me a Advent Calendar, so that I can open a little present every day (as I did for so many years for my family). To bake biscuits and Stollen, and make Christmassy smells of cinnamon and ginger. To cook a goose with all the trimmings – and organise the washing up afterwards. In short, to do all the things that only a woman can do!

Sure, I am a woman myself – and more than capable of doing all the homemaking in the world (after all, I have had nearly 30 years practice). But in the past, I had someone to do it for – a man or a child. Now I have just got me. Mind you, don't think that I am complaining about being a swinging single. No, for most parts of the year it's great fun and egoism pure.

It has one disadvantage, though, and that becomes particularly apparent at the festive season: A woman, who has spent several decades doing things for other people, often finds it difficult to go to the same trouble for herself.

It was no problem to set a fine table and cook a multi-course meal for a loved one. But it is too much bother to light the candles, get out the crystal glasses and do some creative cooking for oneself. When work is pressing and the day long and hard, it is easier to go to a restaurant or put a pizza in the oven. Putting your feet up with a glass of wine is the name of a tired business woman's game!

But I am beginning to think that this is wrong. After all, if one could gain so much pleasure from pleasing a partner, why not enjoy pleasing oneself? Why only take pains for another person? Perhaps looking after 'number one' is more important than I have realised.

A friend of mine told me recently that she sometimes runs the bath, adds dried rose buds, bath oil and swimming candles. Then, enjoying the luxury of chilled champagne in a cooler, she relaxes in the scented water. When I said: "What about the missing ingredient?" She said: "I don't need a man, I do it for myself."

Wow! The mind boggles! I'm not so sure about the rosebuds though, and I might burn some vital part with swimming candles – but that champagne doesn't sound like a bad idea!

MANNERS AND CLOTHES

An interesting English expression is: "Manners maketh man". The German equivalent to this expression with its old English form 'maketh' (makes) is: Kleider machen Leute. Certainly one of the major differences I noticed when I first came to Germany was the emphasis placed on people's clothes, jewellery and outward appearance in general. Although I found the German fashions rather boring (it was 1965 and the height of the Carneby Street era in England) I was certainly impressed by the quality and tasteful colours.

In fact I even went so far as to allow my future sister-in-law to take me to her hairdresser who cut off my long hair and gave me a bouffant style, and to her favourite dress shop where I was rigged out in an elegant grey flannel costume, jumper and pearls (which made me look even older than I do now.)

This attempt to turn me into a German lady was, of course, a total failure – either because I am not a German or not a lady. It certainly did not correspond to my personality as I have never felt easy with the neat-and-tidy, not-a-hair-out-of-place image – although I admire it tremendously when I see it.

I am at my best when I look as if I have just been pulled through a hedge backwards, with every hair going in a different direction and my clothes loose enough to let my energy flow. (Although, dear God, in my next life please make me not only a 'bayerischer Preiß', but also a well-groomed, orderly, never-look-excited version who feels happiest in the straightest of clothes and never wants to wear extravagant Englishy bright colours. OK!?)

No, I am absolutely not a friend of 'grunge', this latest craze of the young, the rich and the famous who take a delight in the deliberate ugliness of sloppy, shapeless, torn and dirty, oversize junk. Quite the opposite, I really appreciate old-fashioned elegance and style, particularly in men. Sure, modern managerial fashion is a delight to the eye if the colours are well-chosen. But I am a fan of the sober-suit brigade, particularly when the suit is a dark back-drop to set off a really way-out tie! In fact, one of my more sober-suited clients gave me such a Freudian flash recently with his crazy-coloured cravat that I – to his great shock – spontaneously threw my arms around his neck (he hasn't dared to wear that tie to his English sessions since!!).

The point I want to make, however, has not to do with clothes but with the English opinion that manners are more important. Although their cheerful disregard of what they are wearing is refreshing, it is not as endearing as their polite, after-you, ladies-first olde worlde etiquette.

Thank God, such 'küß-die-Hand, gnä' Frau' gallantry is not limited to Merry Old England. Because what really turns me on is a combination of both ideals: the well-dressed, well-mannered perfect gentleman!

ENGLISHY BRIGHT

A business friend, whose opinion I value slightly higher than God's, came for one of our regular synergy sessions (I profit from his considerable business experience in return for correcting the rare mistakes in his almost perfect English.)

My new flat has enough space to enable me to use it for training as was the case on this particular evening. Although he has a mega-money palatial home appropriate to his position, I know that he is not a snob and could appreciate the effort I had put into my mini-money, second-hand, painted-over furniture. Like a little puppy wanting to be patted, I waited expectantly for his kind comments. "Very nice. But you should change your candles, they are much too colourful! Typical English taste!"

I immediately valued his opinion slightly less than God's – after all, what is wrong with purple-and-pink candles.
"Why don't you exchange them for beeswax candles?" he suggested tactfully.

"BEESWAX CANDLES ARE BORING!!" I stated categorically. After he had gone, I had to admit that he was right and my beloved candles did look a bit Englishy bright. So I meekly threw them away, put white candles into the grey candlesticks and placed them in my grey-and-white bathroom – a colour scheme which could not offend even the most conservative of Germans (unless they object to my pink towels!).

However, this incident started me thinking about the difference between German and English/American taste. The Germans are renowned for their elegance and perfectly matched colour combinations in clothing and furnishings. We, on the other hand, delight in bright colours and fanciful patterns – the brighter and more fanciful the better! We tend to view the individual article for its intrinsic value, or because we like it and it is useful – and disregard the whole effect.

Once, when my mother was flying home to England, she said: "I'll wear this dress because it doesn't crease (green-and-white striped), these shoes because they are comfortable (brown sandals), this cardigan in case it is cold at the airport (pink) and this scarf (turquoise) in case there is a draught." Although I could follow her logic, I had become so 'German' that I walked ten meters behind her at Fuhlsbüttel airport so that nobody would think that this multi-coloured 'gypsy' was with me!

But in my heart I have retained my English love of colour. Perhaps this is why I like Florida so much where I can wear all the bright clothes I want. Hey, that's an idea! Next time this guy comes, I'll wear my purple-and-pink Disney World outfit (T-shirt and leggings with matching giant earrings and necklace!). That will really blow his mind!

FAT IS FUN!

I must have lost five thousand millions tons of fat during the 54 years that I have been on this planet! Ever since I was thirteen, I have been fighting the battle of the bulge – too little Joan, where Joan should be, and too much Joan everywhere else! (If I ever find the person who decided boobs and butts were sexy but all other part of the body should be fatless, I will personally murder him – or her! Or put differently, long live Rubens!)

And do you know what particularly annoys me? The inequality between men and women! There are all these guys running around, still very attractive in spite of their (small) bellies. But if I looked like that there would be unkind remarks like: "How is it you are pregnant at your time of life?"

Of course, there are those enviable women who never put on weight. Or so they say. "I can eat anything I want!" Huh! They must be related to rabbits because apparently carrots and lettuce leaves are the things they want most. Me – I want chocolate and cake and biscuits and pizza and pasta and thick slices of white bread with lashings of butter and fish and chips and crisps and snacks – all washed down with lots of lovely red wine and the odd drop of whisky!

Oh, it's so unfair! Why is it that all the best things in the world are either illegal, immoral or make you fat? Why can't I find a man who says "The rounder you are, the more there is to love!" Why can't I find clothes which expand to fit the increasing masses? Why can't I be satisfied with being fat and fifty? After all, I will be thin enough to please the most fanatic Twiggy freak after I'm dead!

Of course, I could be like a friend of mine who has decided to choose between eating and drinking all she wants, or finding a new lover – and has rejected the latter. She's happy, munching away on whatever she is offered! She says food (and wine) satisfies her more than any man has!

Or I could listen to the words of Georgina, my cleaning lady from Ghana: "Why are you so thin? You should be fat! Poor women, they are thin! You are rich – you should be fat!" The only problem is that the present state of my bank account would only allow me 2 grams over starvation weight, if it is to be the factor determining my size.

The nicest statement I have heard in a while came from a very wise lady, a few years older than myself: "At our age we have to choose between our bellies and our faces!" Mind you, in my case that is not exactly a brilliant choice! Oh well, where are those damn bathroom scales so I can see, like Garfield, that I am not overweight, I am just under-tall!

THE OLDER THE BETTER!

Age is a funny thing – it is said that you are as old as you feel, but it seems to me that most people feel older than they really are. When I was 19 years old, I looked in the mirror and decided that, as I had aged considerably since I was 18, it was time that I found myself a husband if I didn't want to end up as an old maid sitting on the shelf! So I did! Two months later I had set my sights on a German who came from Hamburg and who wore clothes of a quality I had never seen before, whose father owned six shops and drove a Mercedes.

By the time I was 20, we were engaged – and we were married by the time I was an old lady of 21! I basked in the admiration of all my girlfriends who were amazed at my ability to catch a 'German industrialist' (who spread that rumour!?) and was only a little disillusioned when I discovered that the shops were 'corner shops', the Mercedes was old and rattly – and the high-quality clothes were of Scottish tweed! No matter – I had achieved the dream of all young girls. I had beaten the clock and got a husband before I became a wrinkly hag.

Later, when this marriage ended, I panicked at the thought of having to earn my living alone – after all, I was far too old to start a new life at 38! After nearly 20 years of being a housewife, how was I going to survive in the business jungle? But survive I did, and when I look at the smart, slim, attractive women of around 40, I am amazed that I could possibly have felt old at this 'best time of one's life'.

The worst shock of all came, though, when my daughter came to see me and put a Harley Davidson sticker on the table. "Start saving up – you have until August!" My daughter was referring to the fact that I had said that I would buy a Harley Davidson and a red leather motor-bike suit on the day that I became a grandmother.

Can you imagine how I felt? Me – a grandmother! I immediately started to make my funeral arrangements, take out a life assurance and went to my solicitor to make my will! A grandmother! Now I really am old. Or perhaps not? And anyway – just think of the alternative!

FLIRTING 50's AND SWINGING 60's

Joe Cocker is great! I don't need a therapist, just a visit to one of his concerts. From the very first moment when the announcer says: "I am pleased to welcome the one-and-only Joe Cocker" I am in a megamouth's heaven, screaming my head off (between songs, not while he is singing) for two solid hours, leaving the concert with soaking wet hair, red cheeks, starry eyes, burning hands, sore feet, no voice and a blissful heart!

At a recent concert while we were waiting for Joey to come on stage, I got talking to some of the young people standing next to me. They were probably in their early twenties, and commented that they were very impressed to see several generations in the audience, kids younger than themselves right up to oldies of around fifty (!!??**).
"Sure, I can remember Cocker from Woodstock," I said.
They looked at me in wide-eyed wonder: "Were you actually there – at Woodstock?"

(Oh how I would have loved to have lied! The truth is, I am even older than Woodstock – when Woodstock was happening I was a respectably married housewife and mother, with the swinging years well and truly over!)

"No, I couldn't afford the fare or else I would surely have gone," I answered (God forgive me!).

But that reference to Woodstock and those young people's respect for its memory started me thinking about the good old days – long before Woodstock, and I decided that we 'oldies' have a lot to be proud of!

Do you remember the fifties? Teddy Boys with winkle-picker shoes, brillcreamed hair, boot-lace ties and drain-pipe trousers? It was the time to rock around the clock with Bill Haley; and Elvis the Pelvis was starting to shock parents around the world with his hip gyrations. In England we were dancing to Lonnie Donegan, Tommy Steele – and swooning to Paul Anka's 'Oh, Diana'.

Do you remember the clothes? The first 'grown-up' articles of clothing my mother gave me were a bra (for my non-existent bosom) and an elastic girdle (for my non-existent belly). Oh, the fights that I had with those terrible objects, and with the stockings that I was supposed to attach to the horrible girdle. Actually, it was no wonder that we were chaste! I would rather have died than let a boy see me in my underwear!

Then those petticoats – I used to wear about ten, all washed in sugar water to make them stiff. The problem was in the summer, when the heat made the sugar melt and attracted the wasps! But we cut a good figure, wearing the highest of high heels, wide belts pinching in our waists and skirts swinging as we walked our hip-swaying swagger!

My problem was that it was the era of bosoms, with Marilyn Monroe as a role model. Now, brains I have – bosom I have not (actually, it has apparently been scientifically proven that there is a correlation there somewhere – but that did not comfort me as a teenager when my brain didn't interest me, but my bosom did!)

Of course, I was not the only girl who had this problem and so the market had provided for our needs: you had the choice of either buying a bra three sizes too big and stuffing it with handkerchiefs; or choosing a foam rubber one which stuck out even if it had nothing to fill it; or (as Claudia Schiffer uses today) one which was three sizes too small, had a foam pad underneath and which you pulled up as tight as you could – pushing what little you had into an impressive cleavage.

The problem with the first bra was that you were damned to eternal chastity as it would have been most off-putting for a guy to have to pull out ten handkerchiefs before he could get at you. The second bra had an embarrassing tendency to implode if someone stuck their elbow into you, leaving you with one breast in and one breast out (the worst part was the rude noise it made when it popped back to its original shape). And with the third bra, you couldn't allow yourself to get too excited because it was so tight that you couldn't breathe and would have probably had a heart attack at the vital moment!

Yes, it was the time of 'kissing only, no touching' – we, in our incredible naivety looked askance at the one girl in our school who, as rumour had it, 'had gone all the way' (whatever that meant). Sure, we wore out the back seats of our boyfriends' cars and steamed up a few windows – and although I regularly went to the Saturday-Night Cinema (back row packed, nobody up front) I don't think I ever saw a film right through – but it was harmless fun, and meant that we became artists in turning innocent love-making into a firework of unfulfilled crescendos!

Then, the sixties – probably the most exciting decade of the century. Crying over the deaths of Buddy Holly and James Dean, fighting over the respective merits of Elvis and his me-too copy, Cliff Richard. In 1962, the revolution of those four Liverpudlians who changed the music scene for ever: John, George, Paul and Ringo. Beatlemania in full swing, and those bad guys, 'rubber lips' Mick Jagger with the rest of the Rolling Stones, complaining about their lack of satisfaction and in 'sympathy with the devil'. Moving and impressive, the messages of Joan Baez and Bob Dylan, who showed us that not only can you make music with just a guitar and a voice, but you can also be a force for peace and social change.

Carneby Street, Mary Quant, Twiggy. Throwing away that hated bra and girdle for ever and a day – and welcoming the freedom of either nothing at all or a panty hose, that miracle of clothing which freed up your legs so that you could wear the shortest of minis.

Living off joghurt and crisp bread, with anorexia just around the corner, the main thing to be 20 kilos underweight (thank God, bosoms were out!) Long hair swinging straight down your back, like Sandy Shaw – even, like her, going barefoot in good weather. False eyelashes and eyeliner making your eyes seem bigger than your face. Moving freely with the music. Finding your first serious boyfriend and finally, after months of opening frontiers, shyly discovering with this your unforgettable first love what love is all about.

Yes, we of the 'sixties' are now the 'fifties' of today! But didn't we have a great time? Wasn't it fun? And it is fitting that in 1969, Woodstock was to sound the final chord on this age of innocence, opening the way for the flower-power, drugs-sex-and-rock-and-roll, make-love-not-war era of the seventies. But I'm too old to remember that!

POWERCHICKS

In the Financial Times recently, Lucy Kellaway wrote a delightful review of "a resolutely upbeat book that claims women are poised to dominate the US." Powerchicks is a new book about women in the US – written by a man. A white, Southern, middle-aged man called Matt Towery, The cover shows just such a "powerchick", her broad shoulders, spiked heels and briefcase silhouetted against the rising sun and orange sky.

Mr. Towery offers 10 "powerpoints" for the would-be powerchick:

Powerpoint 1 is to be proud to be a woman (as Lucy Kellaway mockingly comments: this must be an American idea, as a Brit would no more think to be proud of being a woman than being 5ft. 4ins. or having brown hair).

Powerpoints 2 to 10 include being decisive, being a team player, being flexible and creative, communicating well, taking risks and having a mission.

Ms. Kellaway comments: "Thinking about these I find I know lots of perfect powerchicks. The trouble is, more than half of them are men." (What would they be called? Powercocks? – Joan's comment)

She finishes by quoting the author's account of asking a successful woman whether she objects to being referred to as a powerchick and who screams at him: "Hell, no!"

Although her witty review cheered up my flight to Hamburg, it got me thinking about the whole phenomenon of successful women and their new identity. Watching powerful women on television, whether businesswomen, politicians or whatever, I often get the feeling that they have lost their femininity to become rather poor copies of men (or am I being chauvinistic?).

Actually, this has got me rather worried as my own daughter, an anthropologist, commented some time ago that it was interesting for her to detect the "mannerisms of power and authority" in my body language "which one would normally only associate with successful men".

Is it really a contradiction in terms for a woman to be successful? To be powerful, dominating, a leader of men? To exert her opinion, withstand pressure, and where necessary even subjugate the opposition? Does this automatically mean a denial of her basic role in life – her womanhood? Or is it a return to what nature intended – to the "ancient goddess", the matriarchal society?

To be quite honest, I don't know. Personally, I spent years unsuccessfully attempting to be weaker than the men in my life so that I wouldn't frighten them away. After all, I was brought up in a strictly religious home with the biblical command that the woman is to be submissive to the man as she would be to God because the man is the head of the woman. For decades I believed that this was the order of things.

Even today after having left such bigotry behind me, I am still not attracted by the aggressive, anti-man attitude of the "bra-burners". I like being a woman too much. I like men too much. Particularly those who by nature – not by artificial status – are stronger than me.

But of one thing I am certain – "Cowboy Joan" I may be. "Powerchick" I am not.

ISBN 3-9806075-8-5

Alle Rechte vorbehalten:
© by Joan von Ehren 2000
YES! Your English Services
Groten Flerren 24, D-22559 Hamburg
Tel.: +49 (0)40/819 932 - 0, Fax: +49 (0)40/819 932 – 29
Email: Office@yes-net.de, Internet: www.yes-site.com

Alle Rechte der Gesamtausgabe:
© RosenfeldKommunikation GmbH Frankfurt/Main München 2000
Wilhelm-Leibl-Str. 3, D-81479 München
Tel.: +49 (0)89/74997472, Fax: +49 (0)89/74997473
Email: info@rosenfeld.cc

Vignetten: Imke Kretzmann, Hamburg
Umschlagfoto: Rolf Nachbar, Albertshausen
Lithos: DeSoto, Wiesbaden
Druck und Bindung: Fotolito Longo, Bozen

Printed in Italy